FOR ORGANS, PIANOS & ELECTRONIC KEYBOARDS

209

Christmas Favorites

E-Z Play TODAY chord notation is designed for playing **standard chord positions** or **single key chords** on all **major brand organs** and **portable keyboards**.

Contents

7777 W. BLUEMOUND RD. P.O. BOX 13819 MILWAUKEE, WI 53213

2

All Through The Night

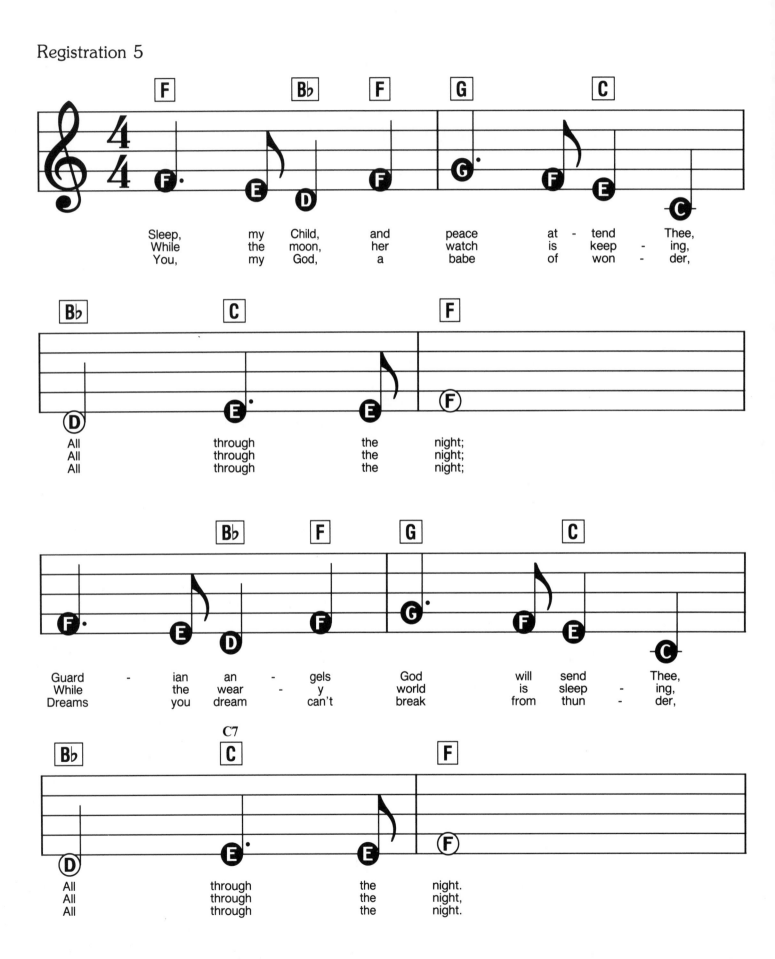

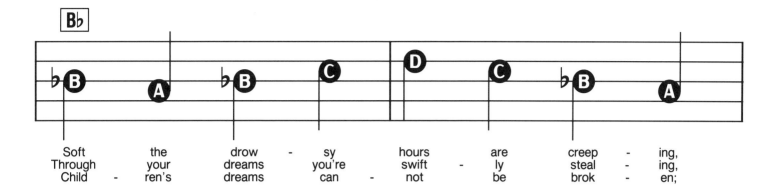

Soft   the   drow   -   sy   hours   are   creep   -   ing,
Through   your   dreams   you're   swift   -   ly   steal   -   ing,
Child   -   ren's   dreams   can   -   not   be   brok   -   en;

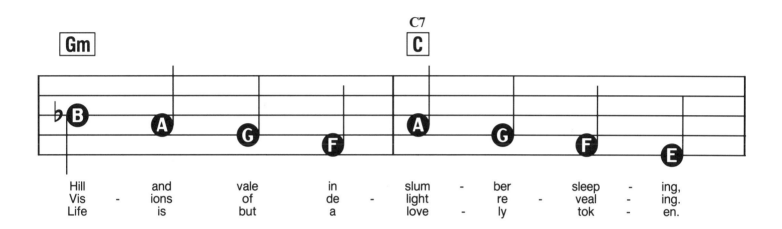

Hill   and   vale   in   slum   -   ber   sleep   -   ing,
Vis   -   ions   of   de   -   light   re   -   veal   -   ing.
Life   is   but   a   love   -   ly   tok   -   en.

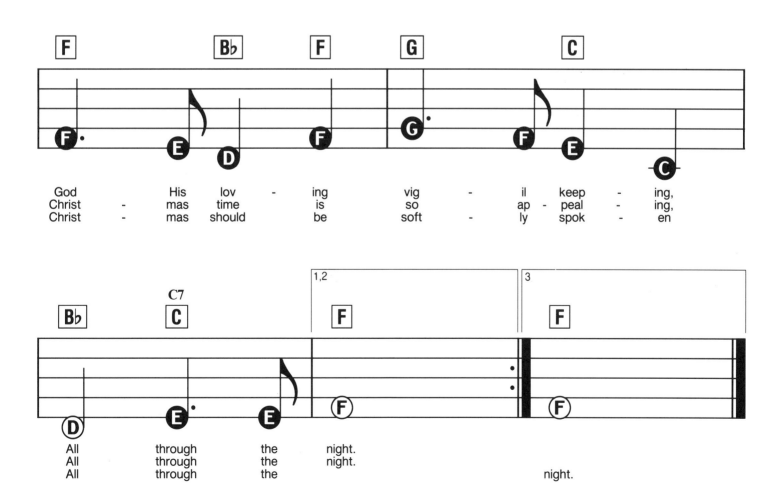

God   His   lov   -   ing   vig   -   il   keep   -   ing,
Christ   -   mas   time   is   so   ap   -   peal   -   ing,
Christ   -   mas   should   be   soft   -   ly   spok   -   en

All   through   the   night.
All   through   the   night.
All   through   the   night.

As Lately We Watched

Registration 1

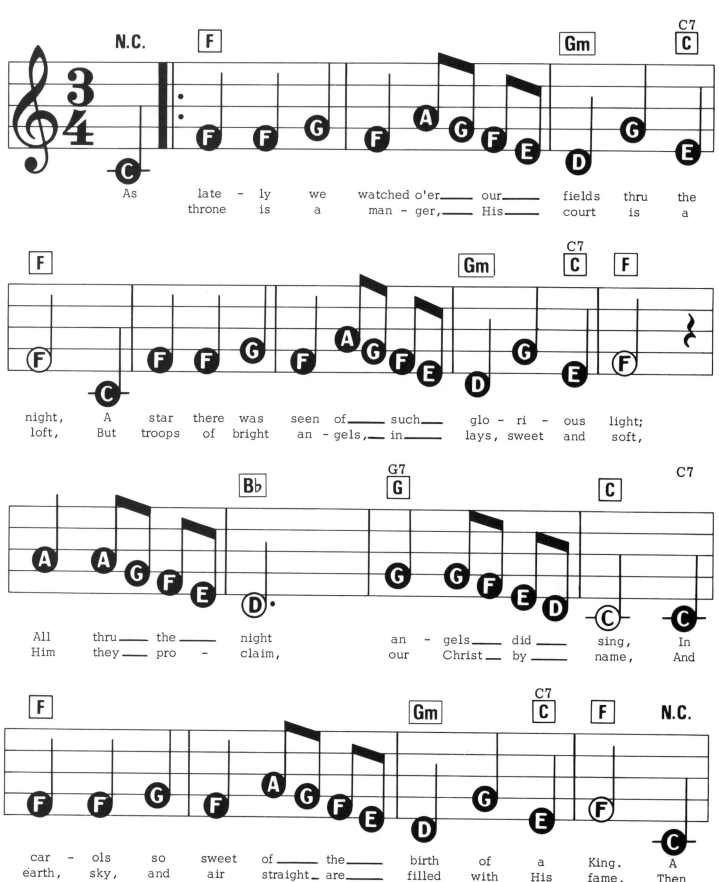

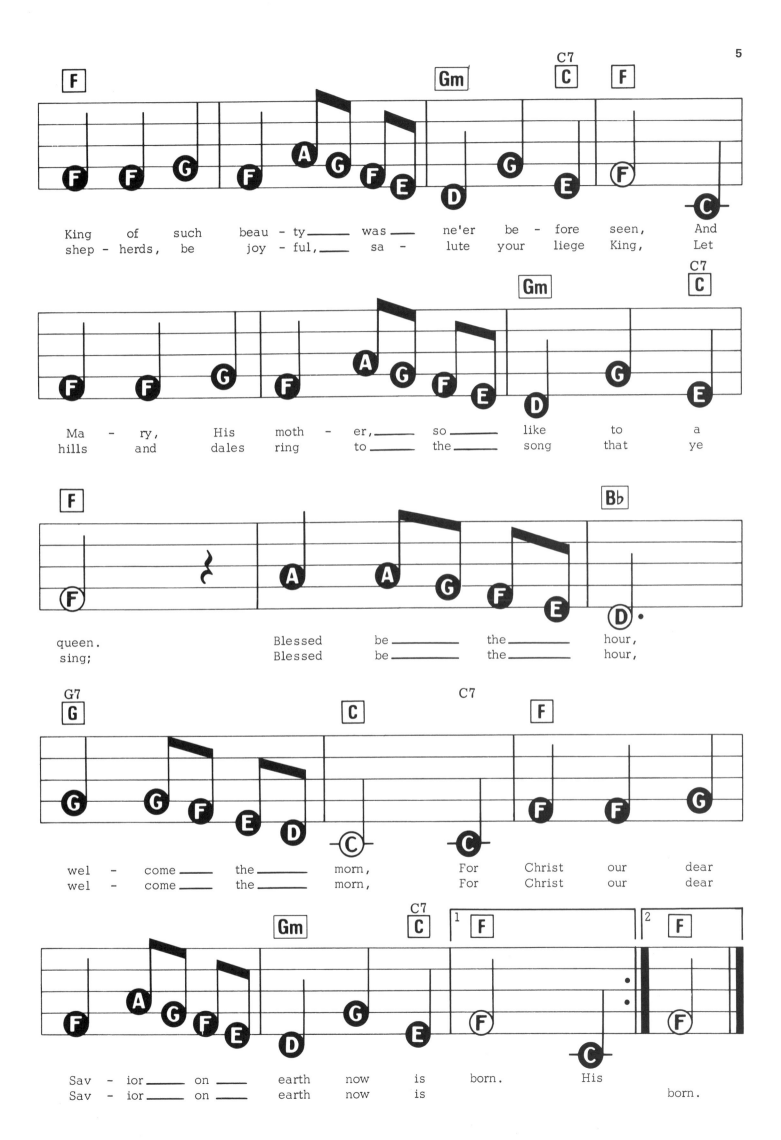

Angels We Have Heard On High

Registration 3

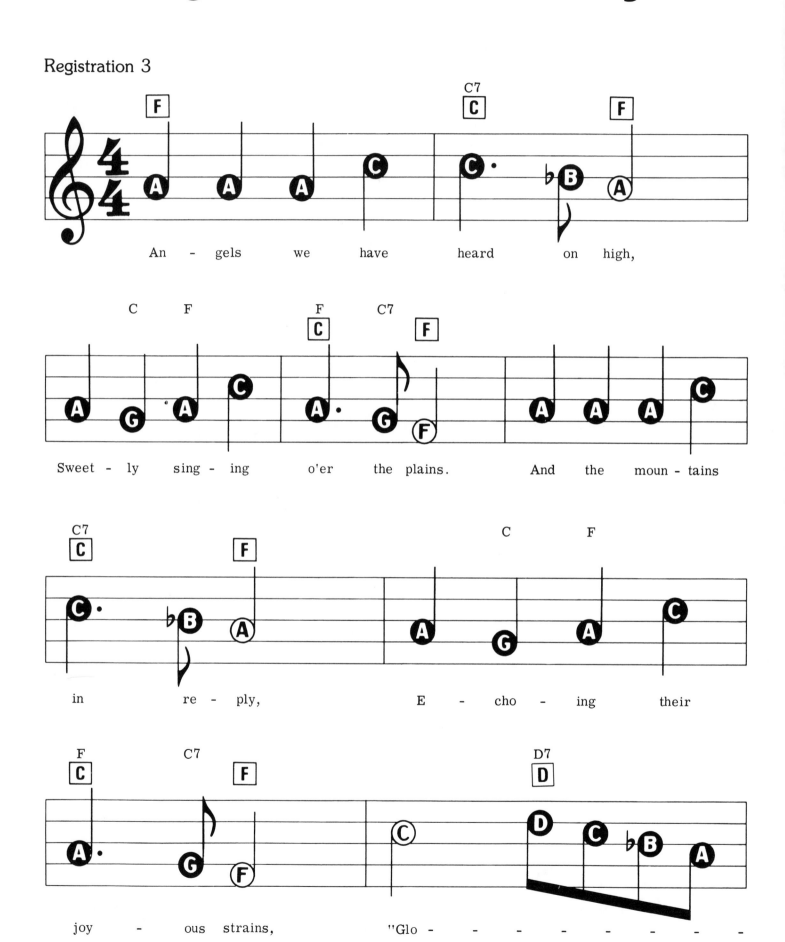

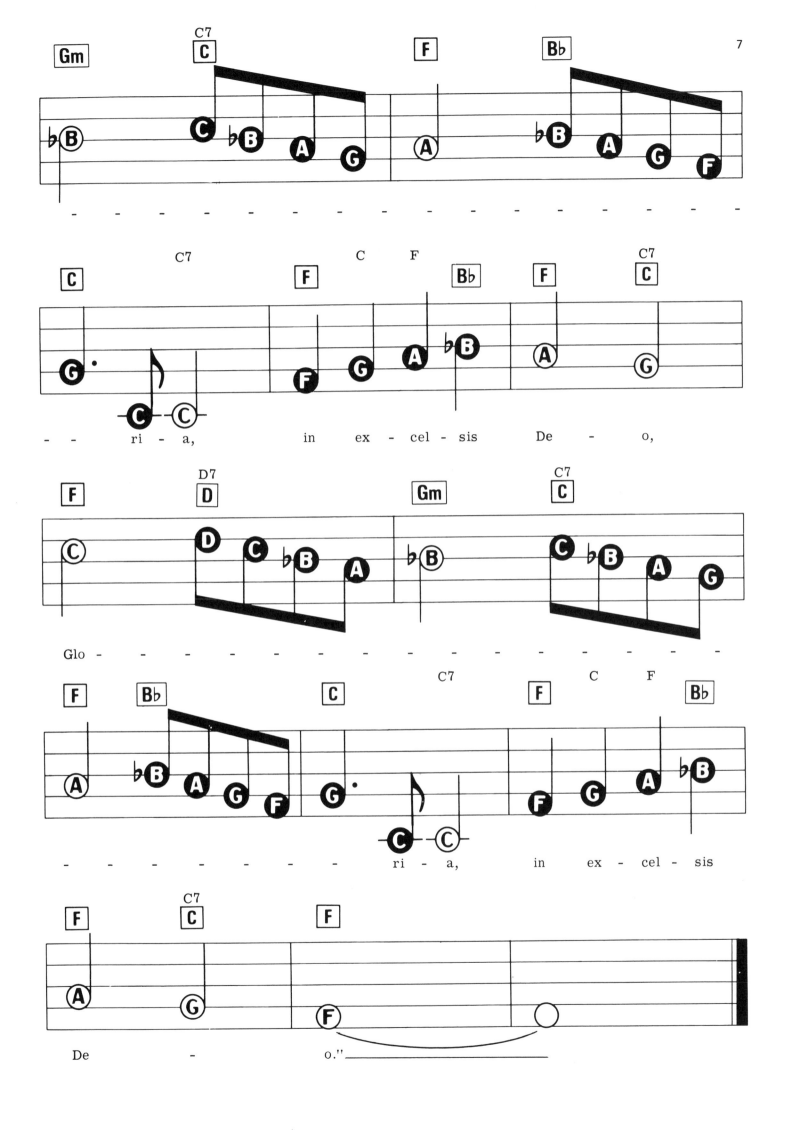

Away In A Manger

Registration 1
Rhythm: Waltz

Luther/Spillman

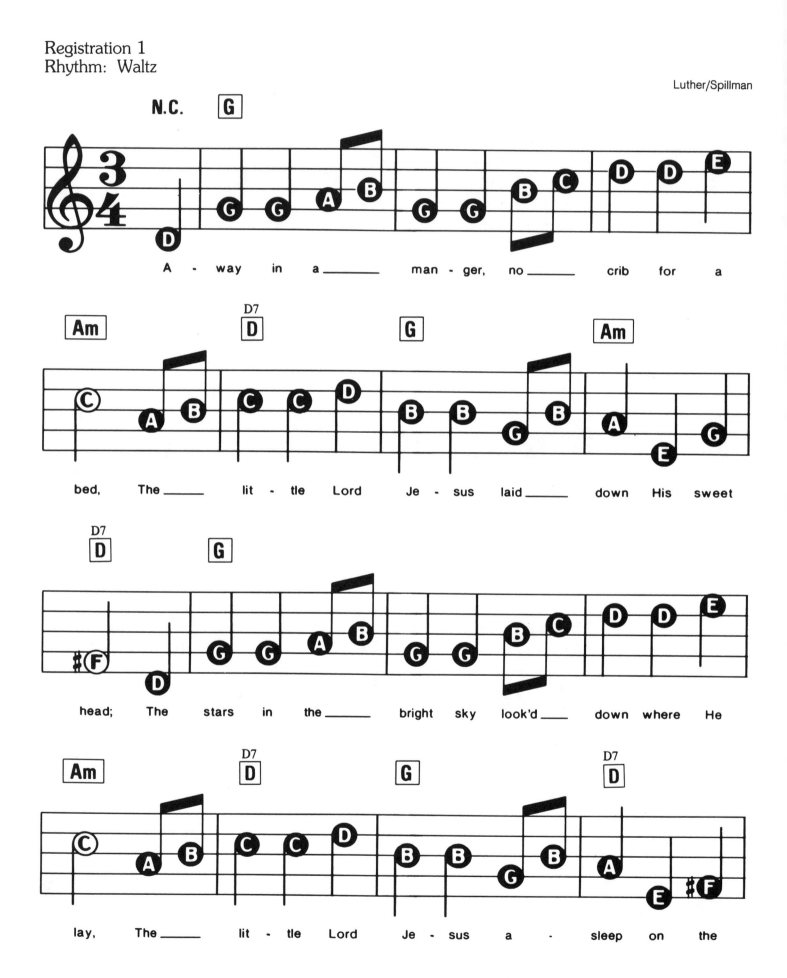

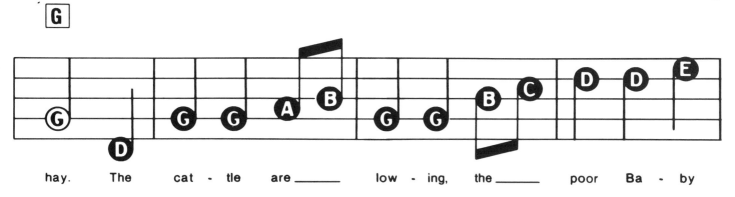

hay. The cat - tle are _____ low - ing, the _____ poor Ba - by

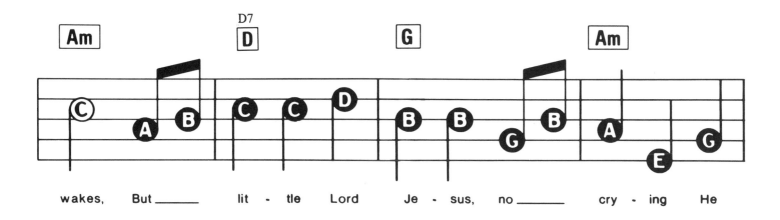

wakes, But _____ lit - tle Lord Je - sus, no _____ cry - ing He

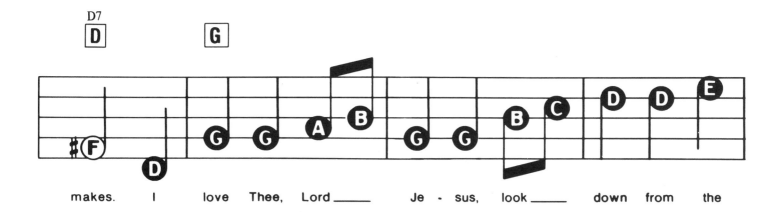

makes. I love Thee, Lord _____ Je - sus, look _____ down from the

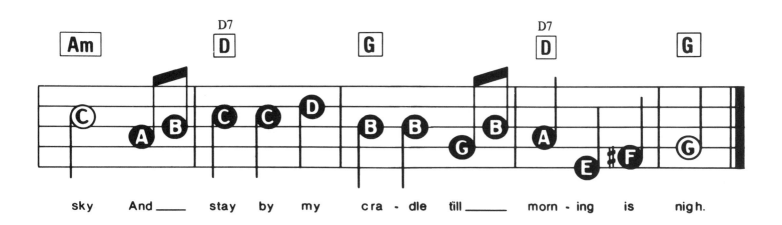

sky And _____ stay by my cra - dle till _____ morn - ing is nigh.

I Saw Three Ships

Registration 2

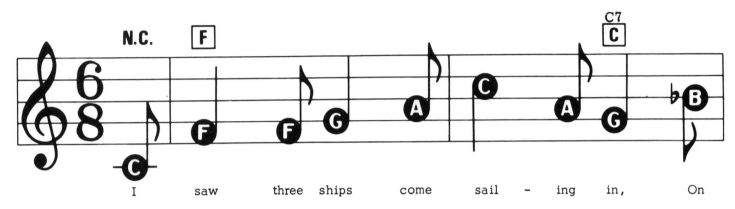

I saw three ships come sail - ing in, On

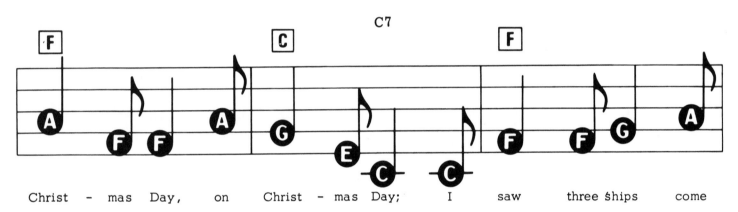

Christ - mas Day, on Christ - mas Day; I saw three ships come

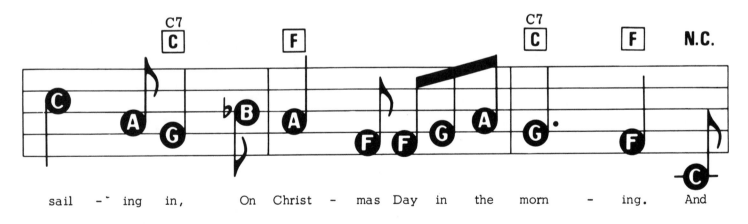

sail - ing in, On Christ - mas Day in the morn - ing. And

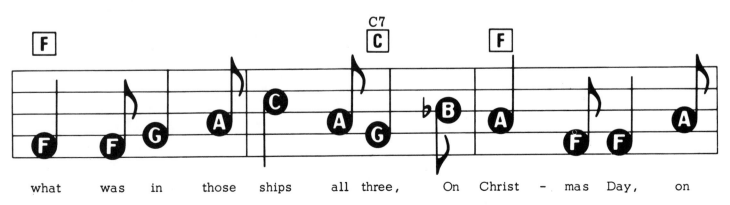

what was in those ships all three, On Christ - mas Day, on

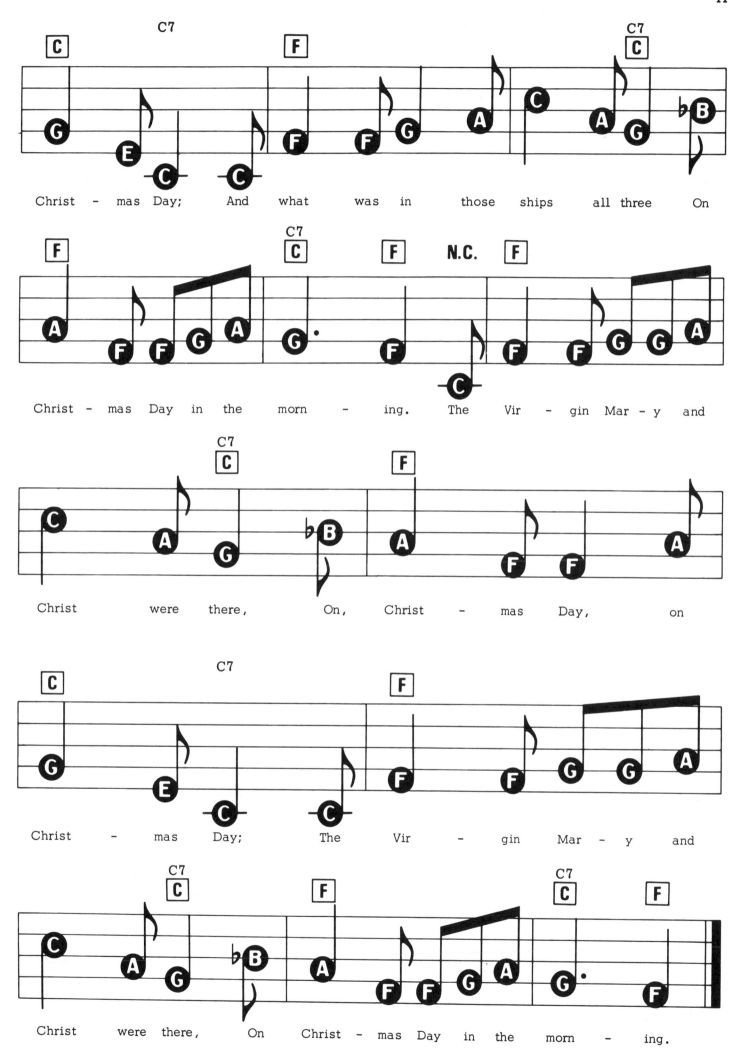

Deck The Hall

Registration 5

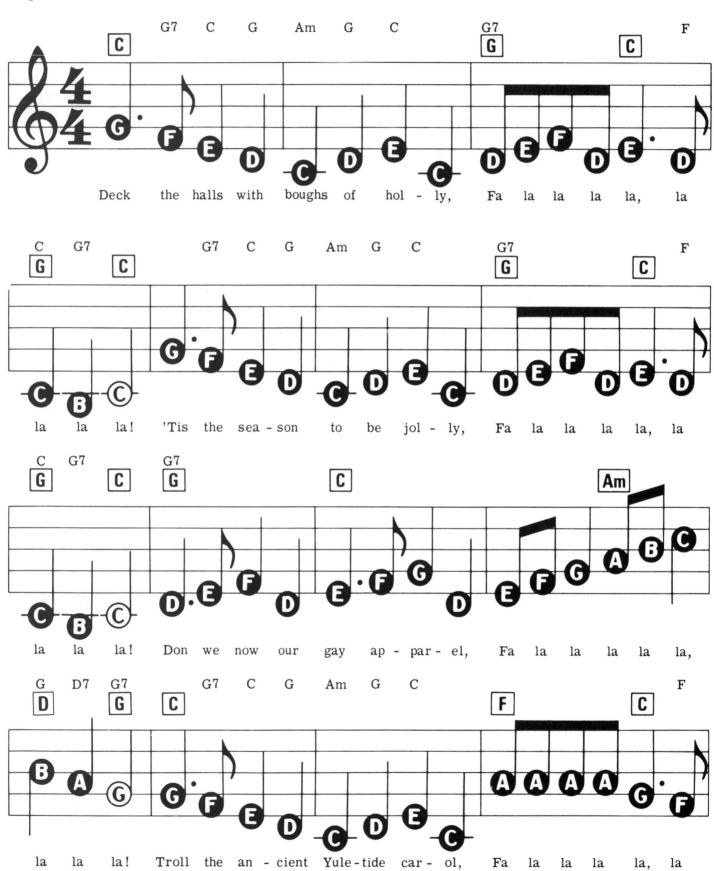

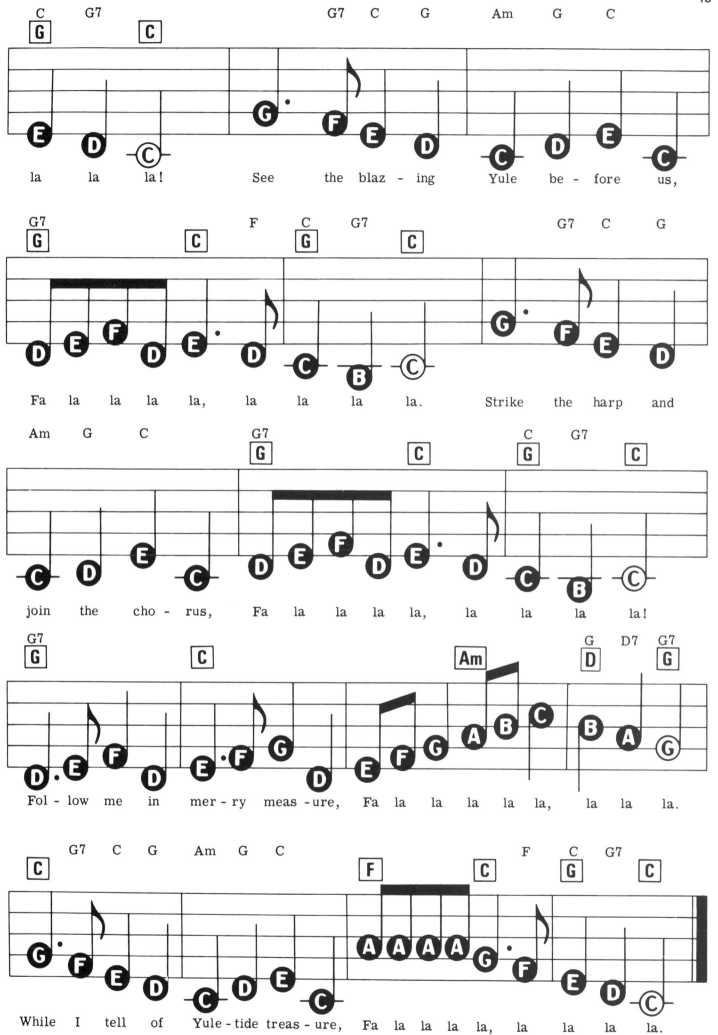

13

The Friendly Beasts

Registration 2

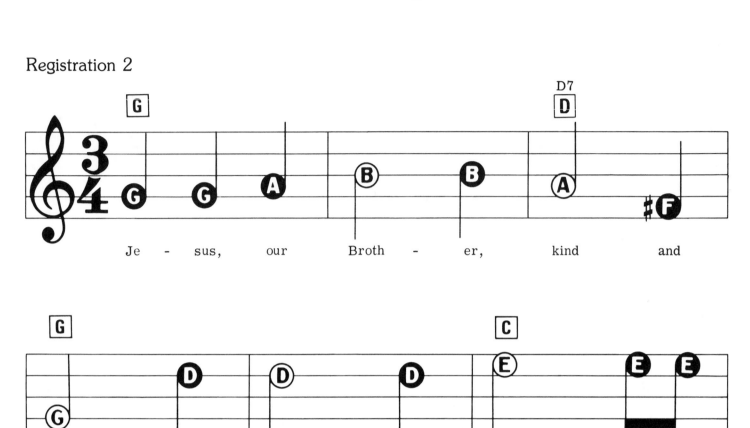

Je - sus, our Broth - er, kind and

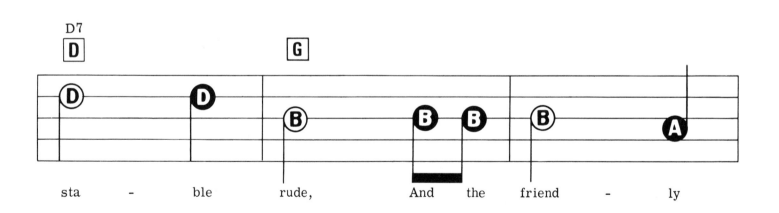

good, Was hum - bly born in a

sta - ble rude, And the friend - ly

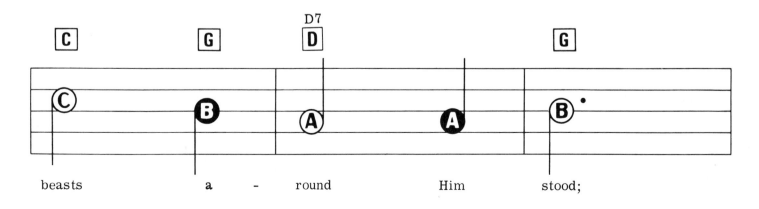

beasts a - round Him stood;

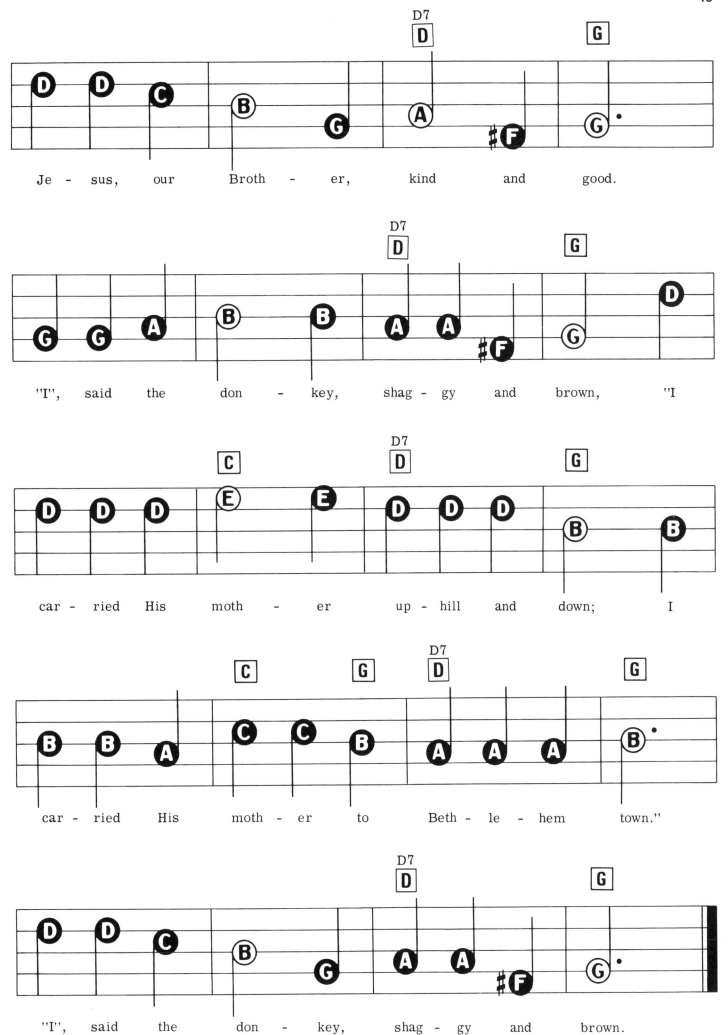

Gather Around The Christmas Tree

Registration 3

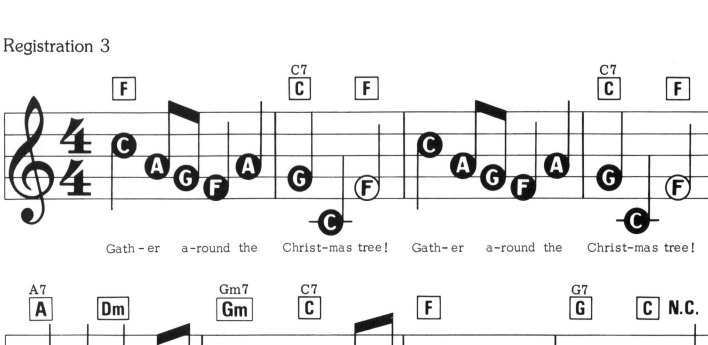

Gath - er a-round the Christ-mas tree! Gath- er a-round the Christ-mas tree!

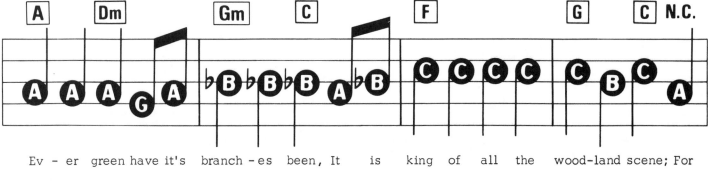

Ev - er green have it's branch - es been, It is king of all the wood-land scene; For

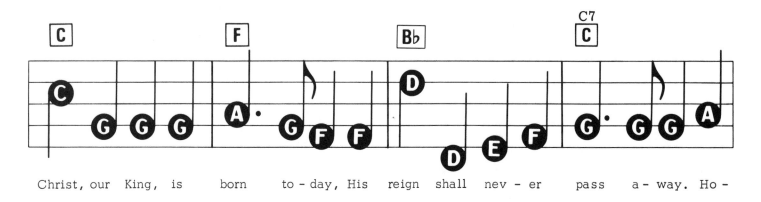

Christ, our King, is born to - day, His reign shall nev - er pass a - way. Ho -

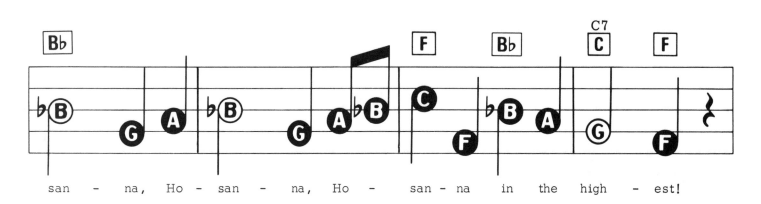

san - na, Ho - san - na, Ho - san - na in the high - est!

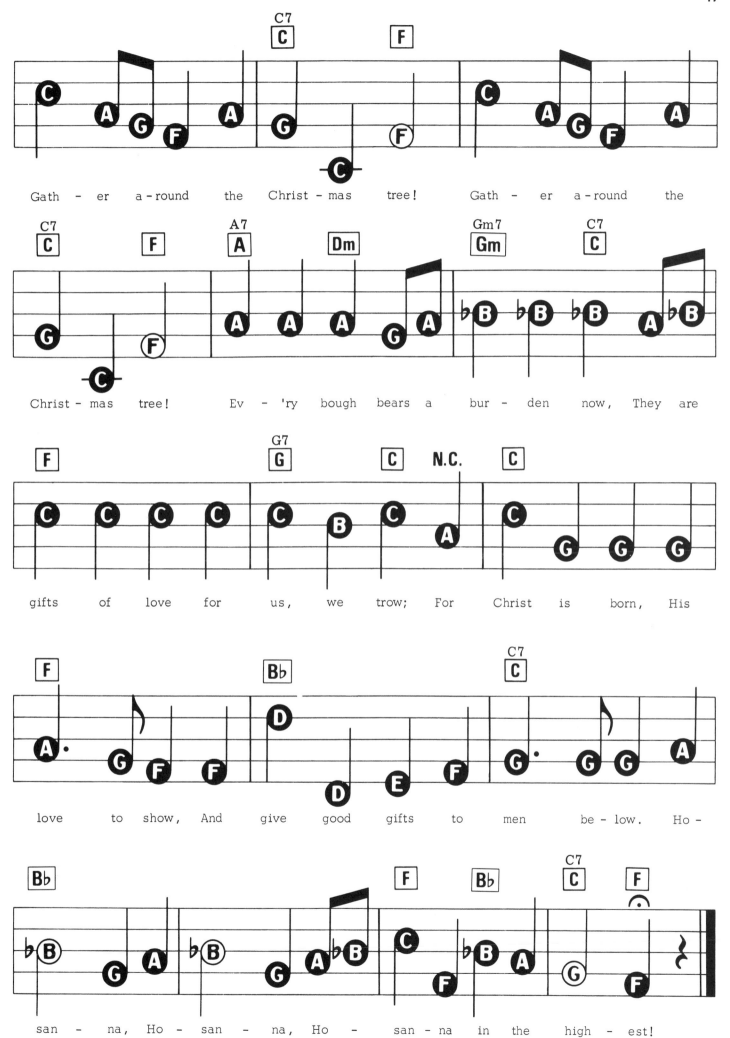

Go Tell It On The Mountain

Registration 5
Rhythm: Jazz or Swing

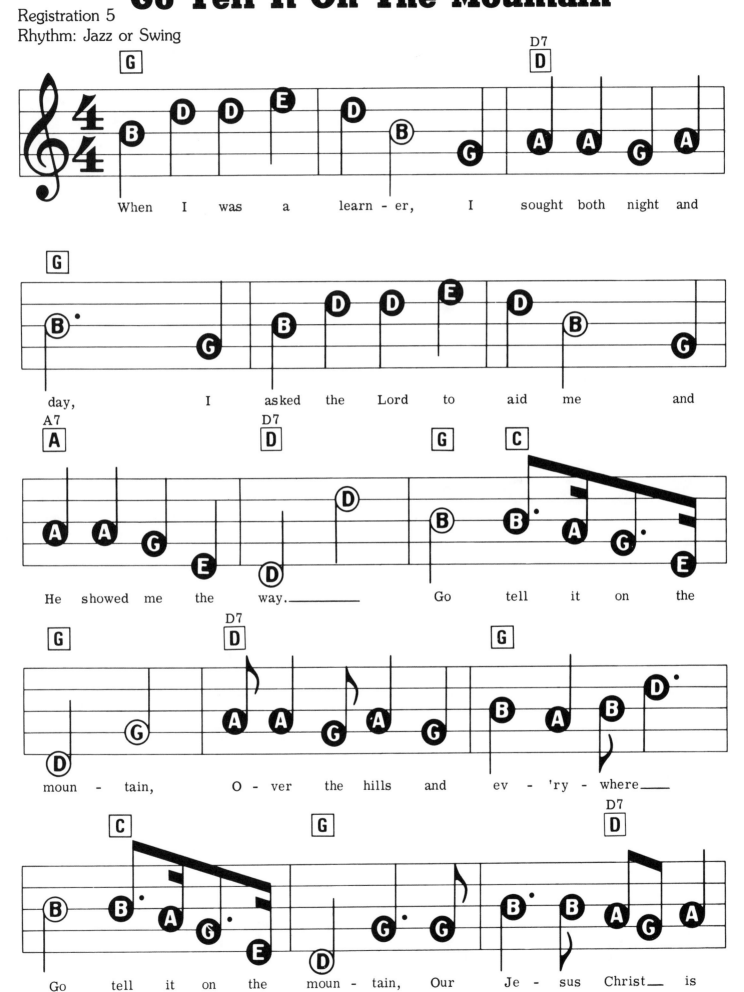

19

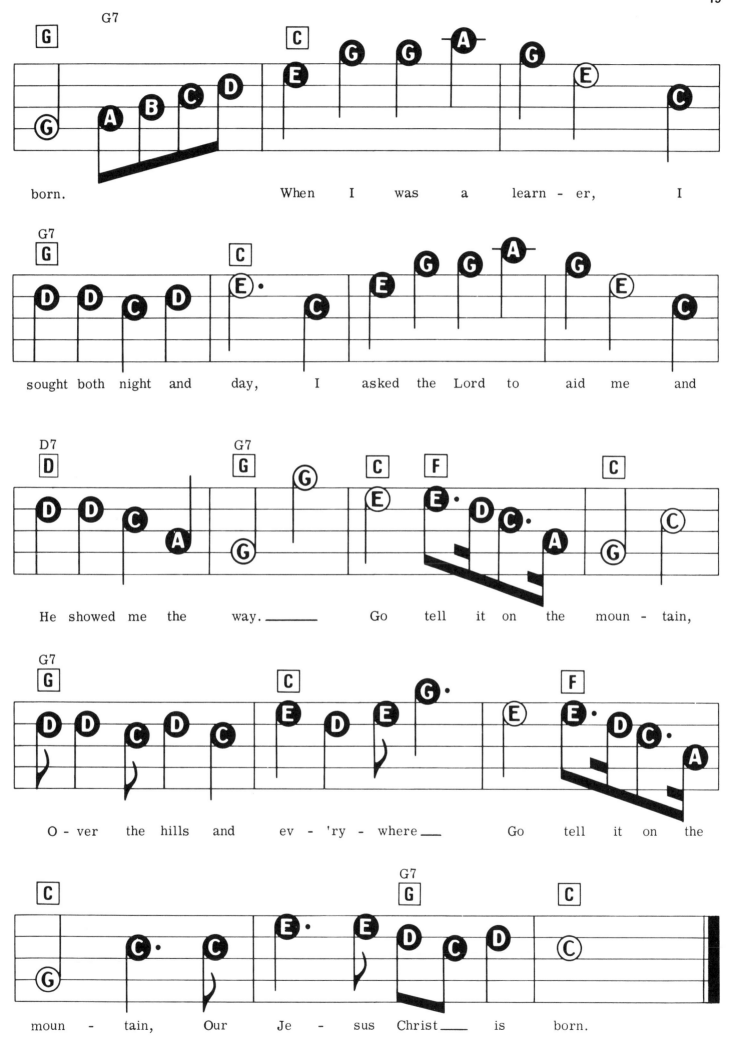

God Rest Ye Merry, Gentlemen

Registration 6

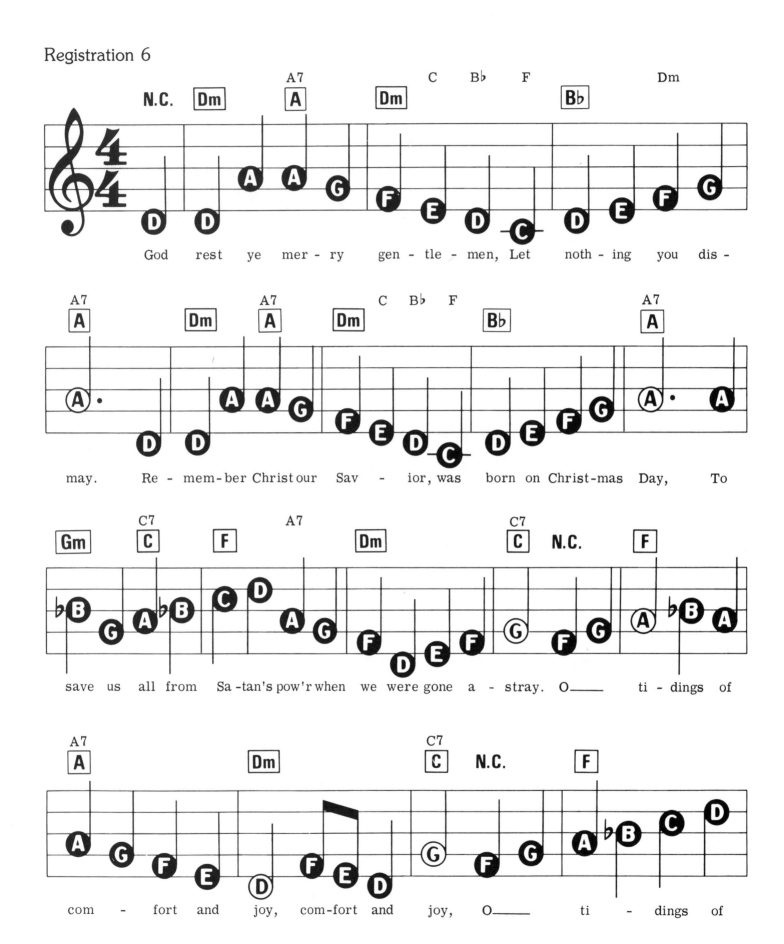

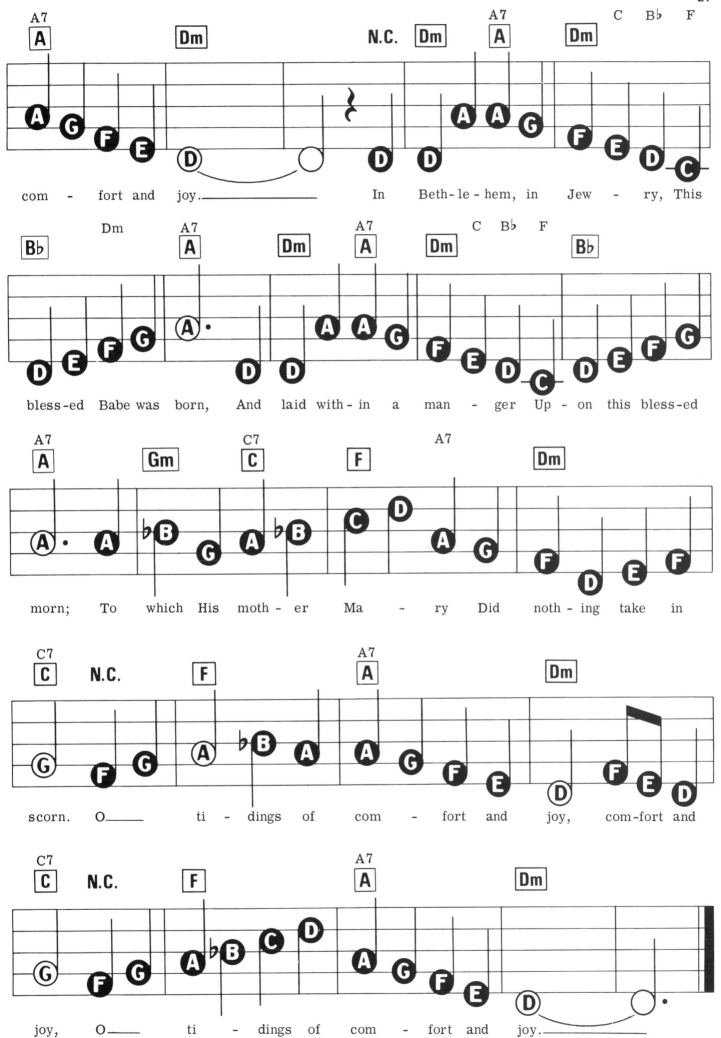

Hark! The Herald Angels Sing

Registration 5

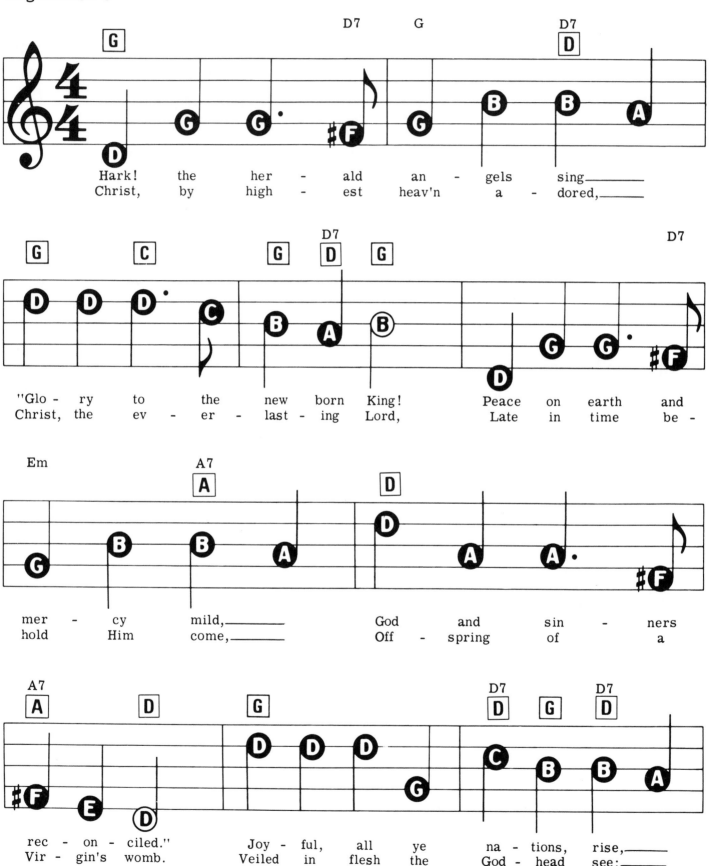

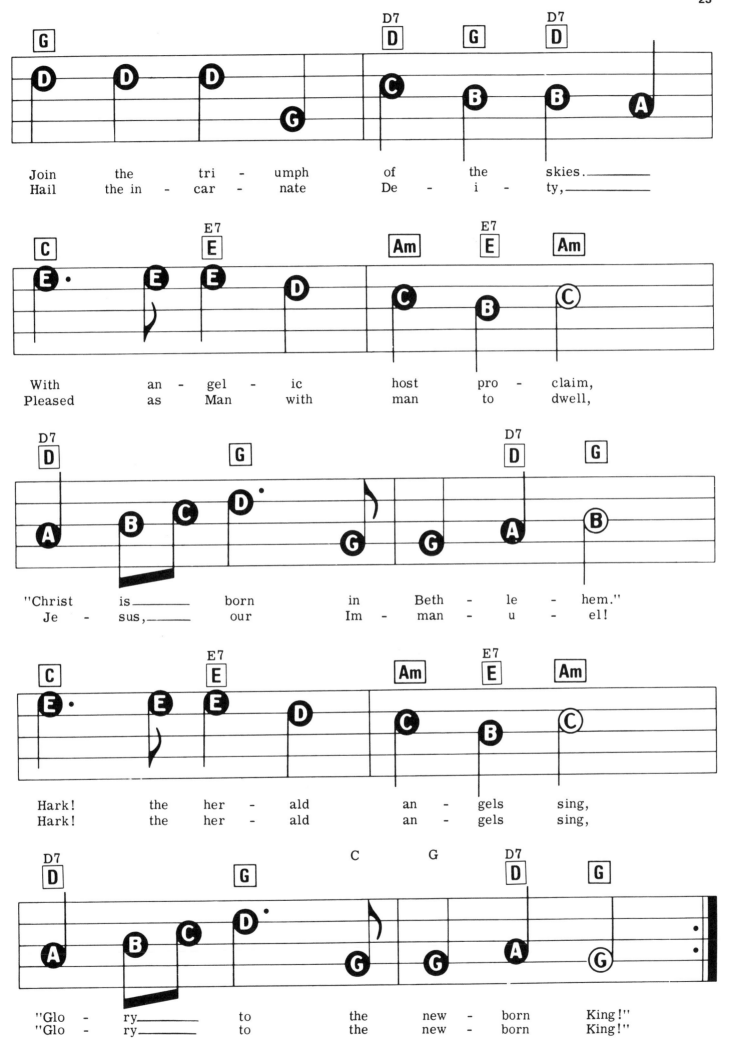

Here We Come A-Wassailing

Registration 3

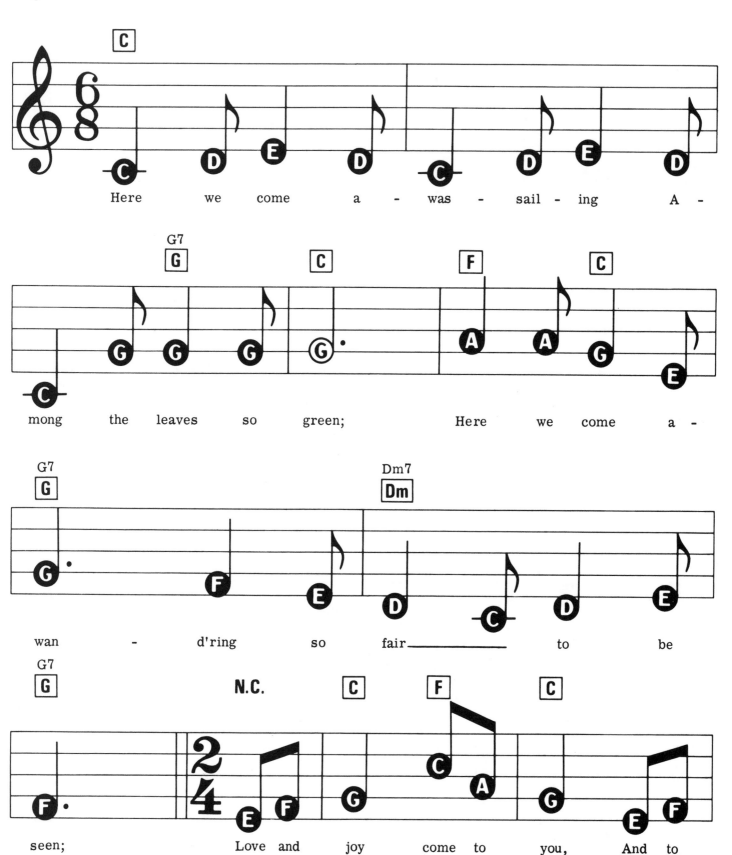

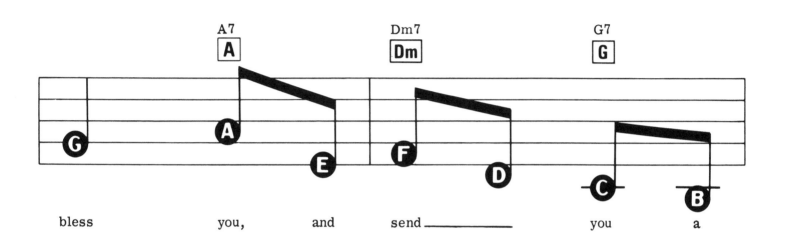

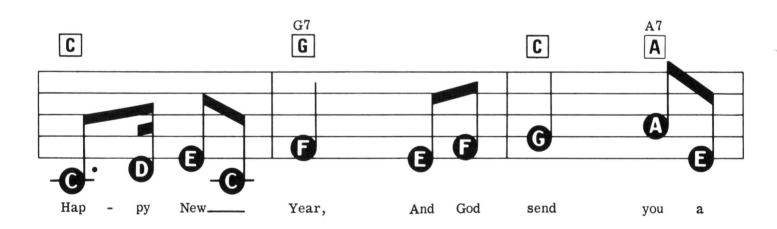

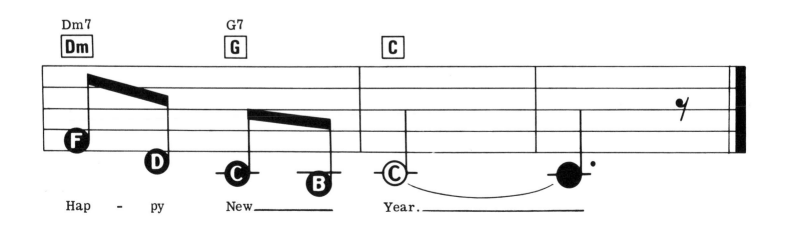

It Came Upon The Midnight Clear

Registration 1

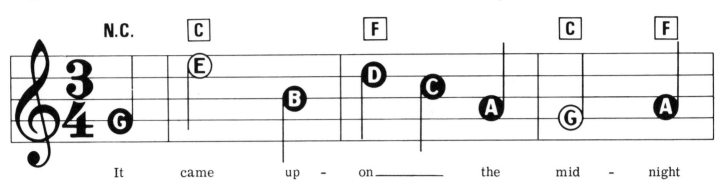

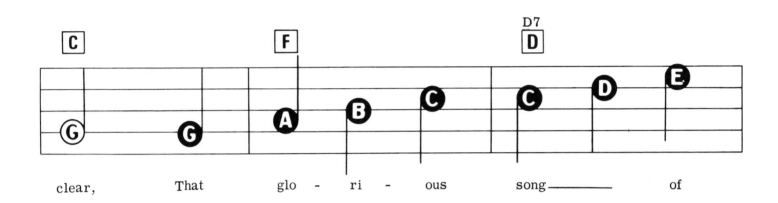

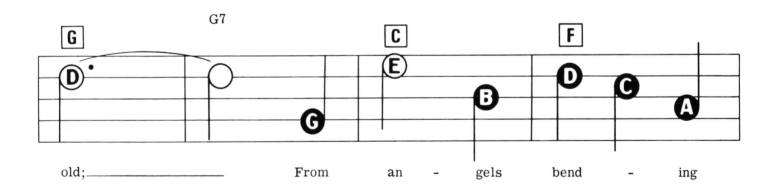

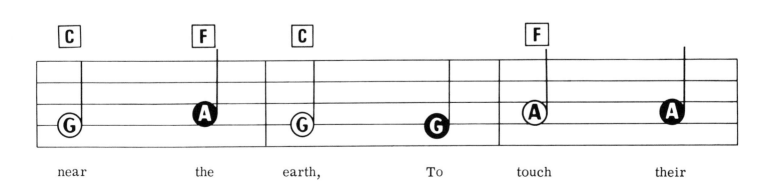

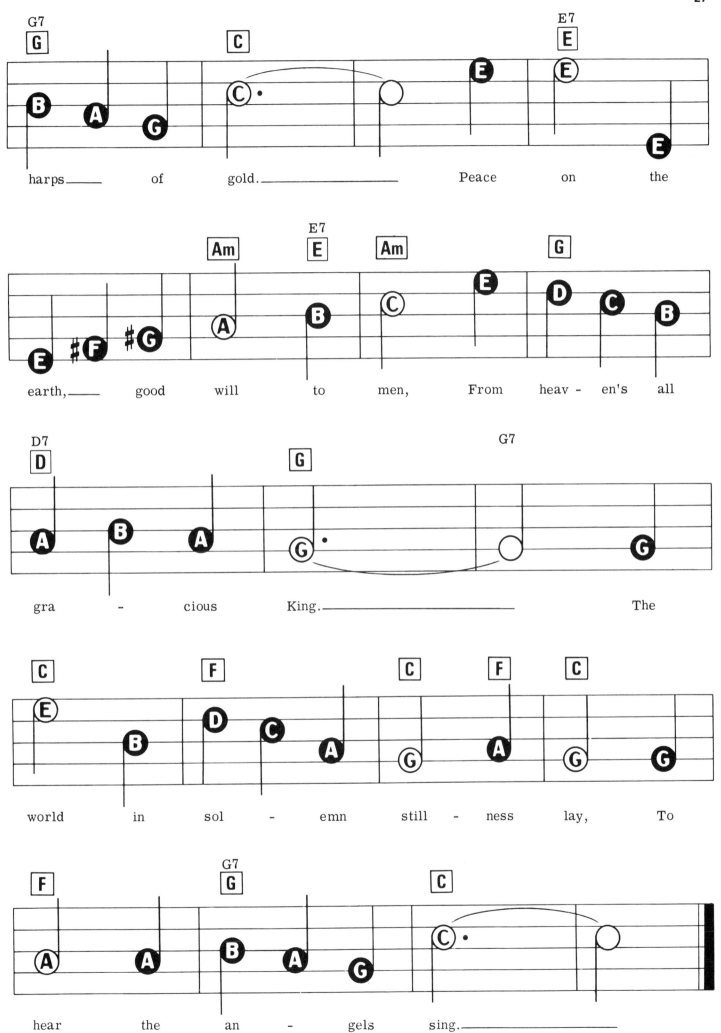

Jingle Bells

Registration 5
Rhythm: Fox Trot or Swing

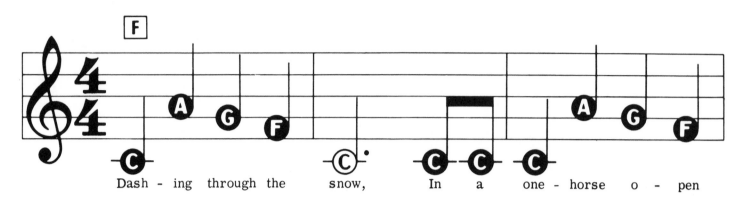

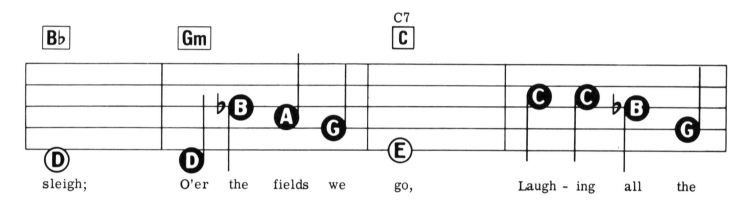

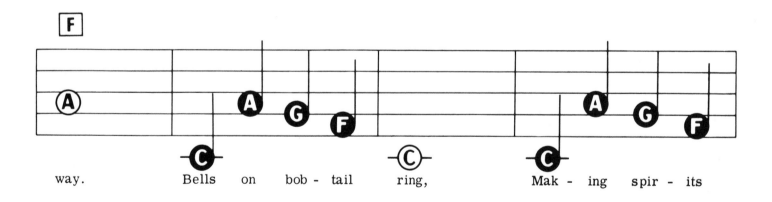

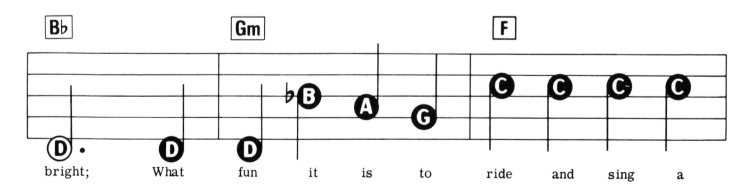

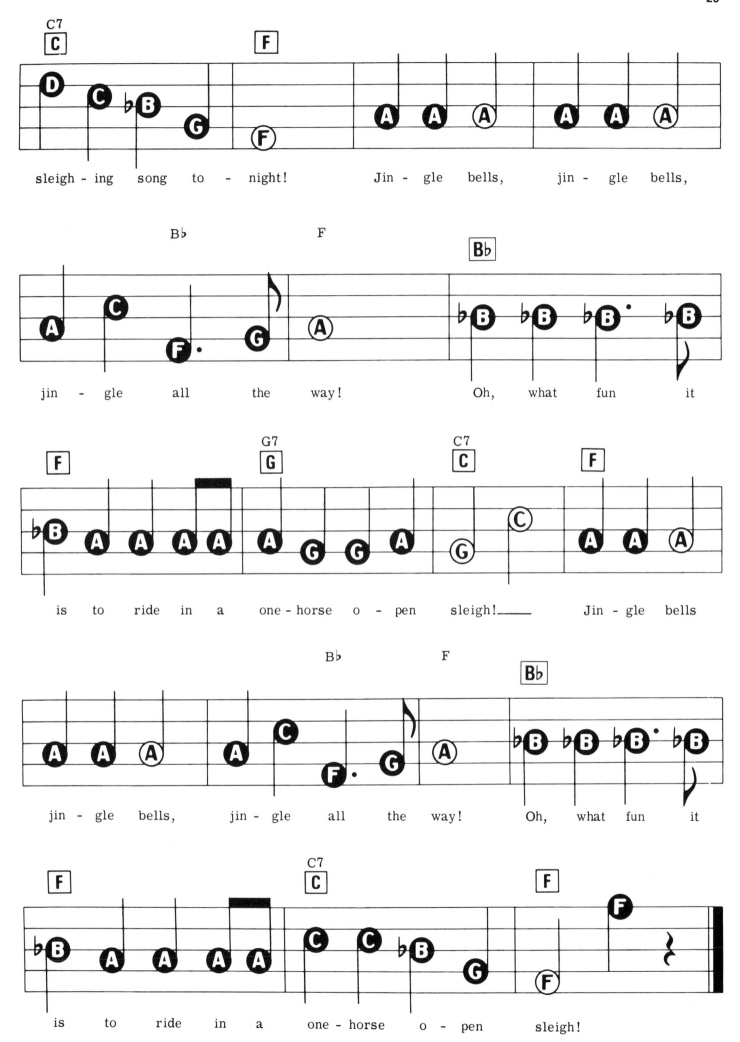

O Christmas Tree

Registration 3

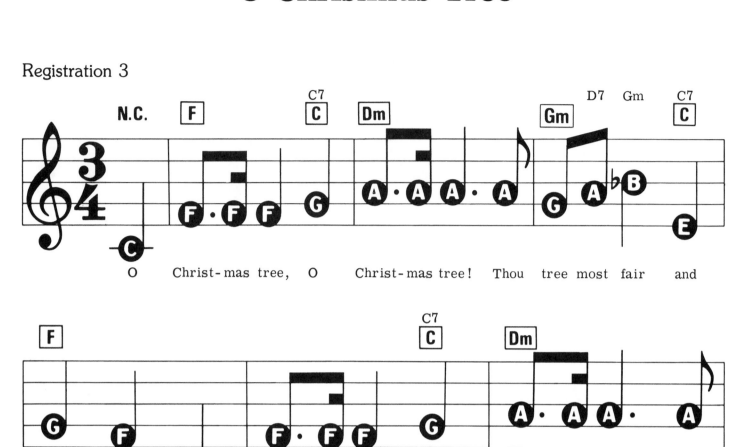

O Christ-mas tree, O Christ-mas tree! Thou tree most fair and

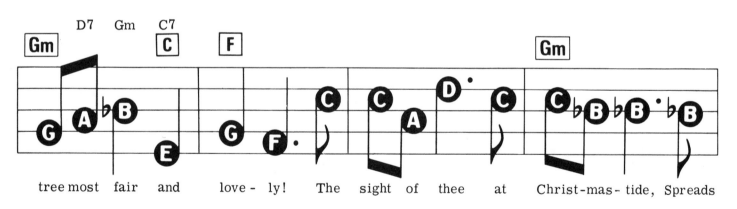

love - ly! O Christ - mas tree, O Christ - mas tree! Thou

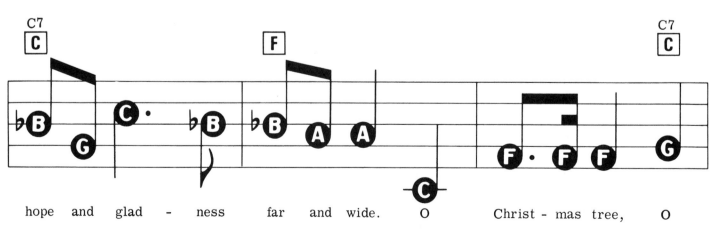

tree most fair and love - ly! The sight of thee at Christ-mas- tide, Spreads

hope and glad - ness far and wide. O Christ - mas tree, O

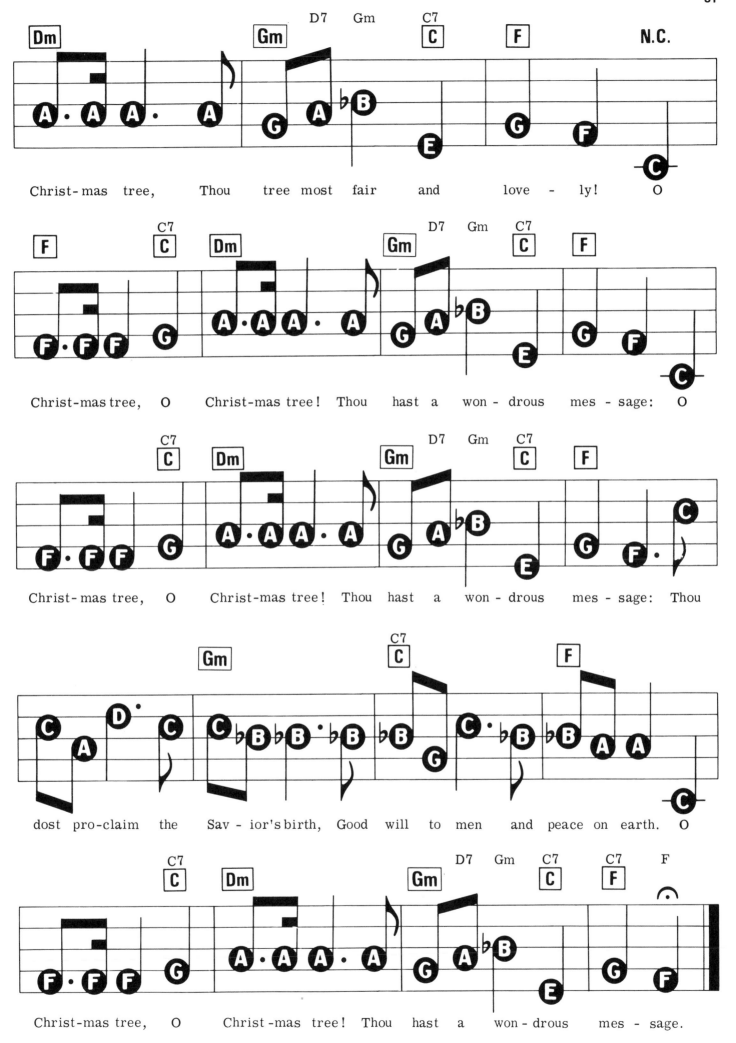

O Come All Ye Faithful

Registration 6

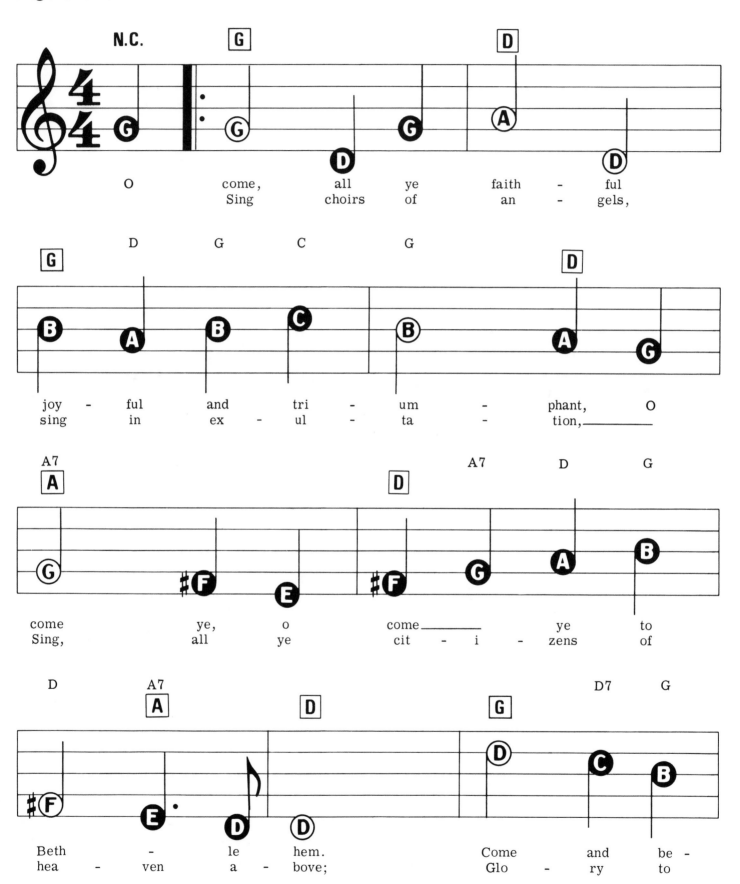

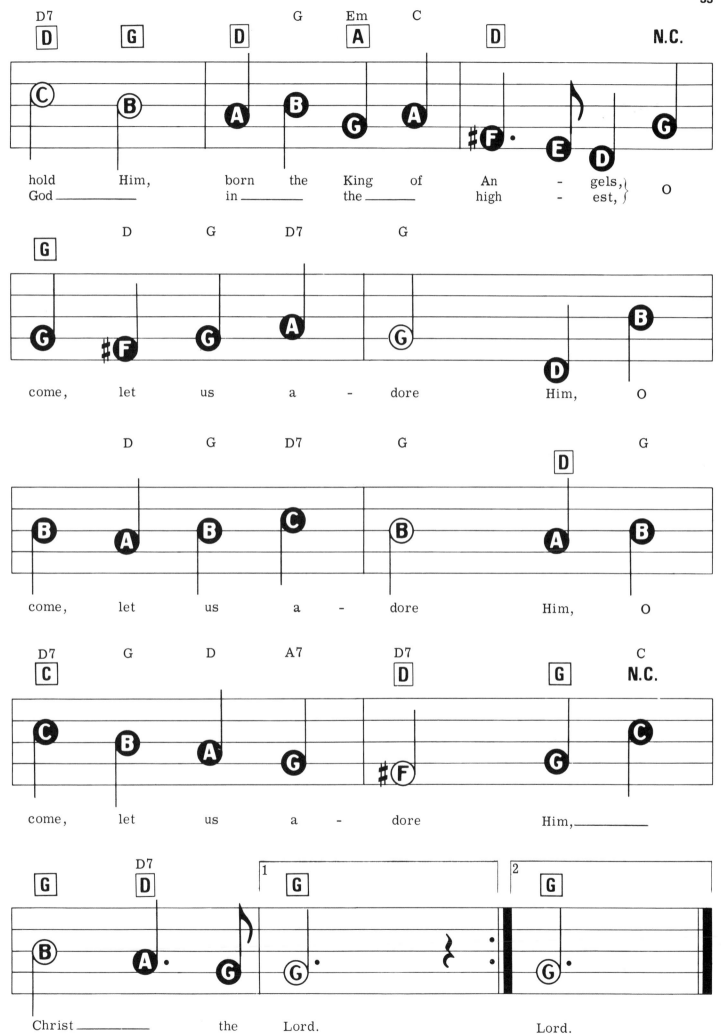

O Come, O Come Emmanuel

Registration 3

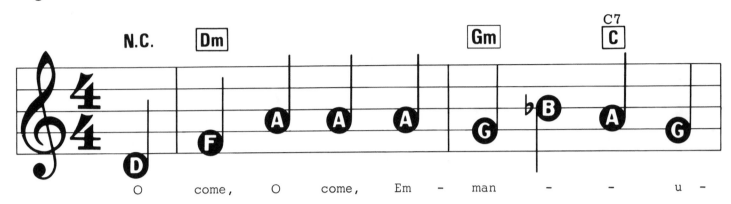

O come, O come, Em - man - - u -

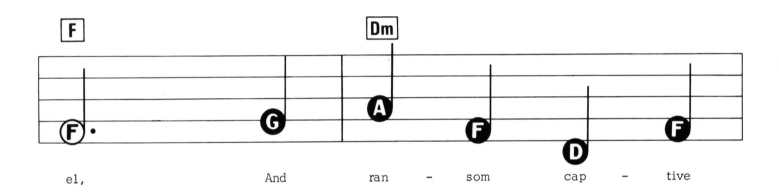

el, And ran - som cap - tive

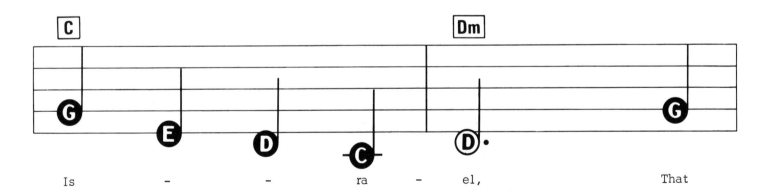

Is - - ra - el, That

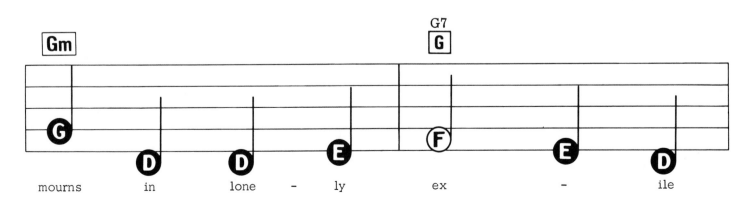

mourns in lone - ly ex - ile

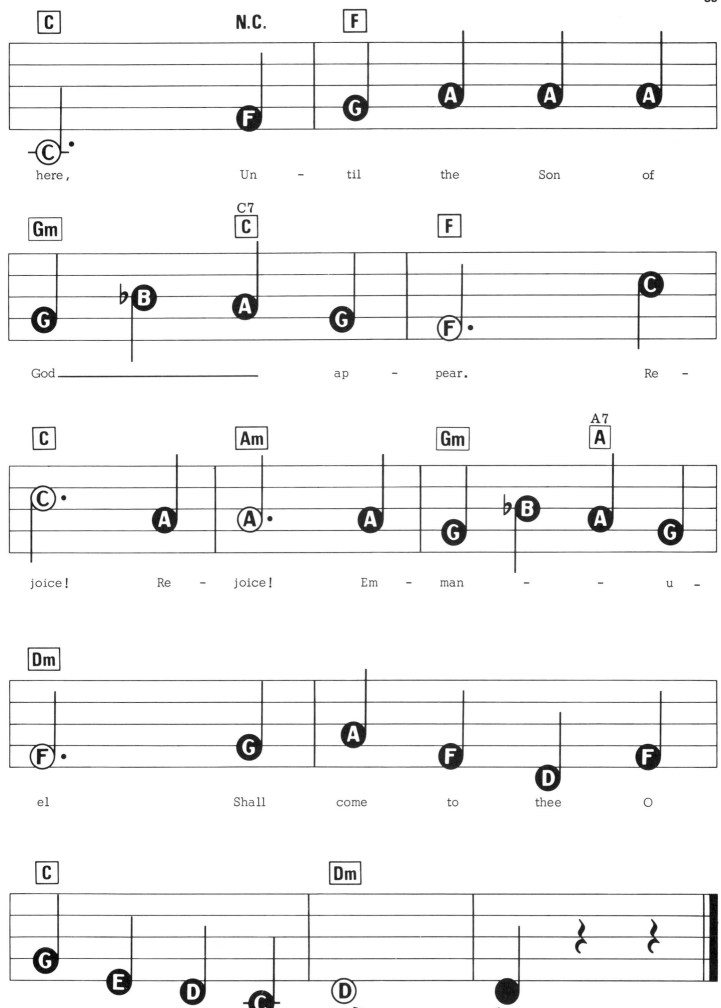

Silent Night

Registration 1

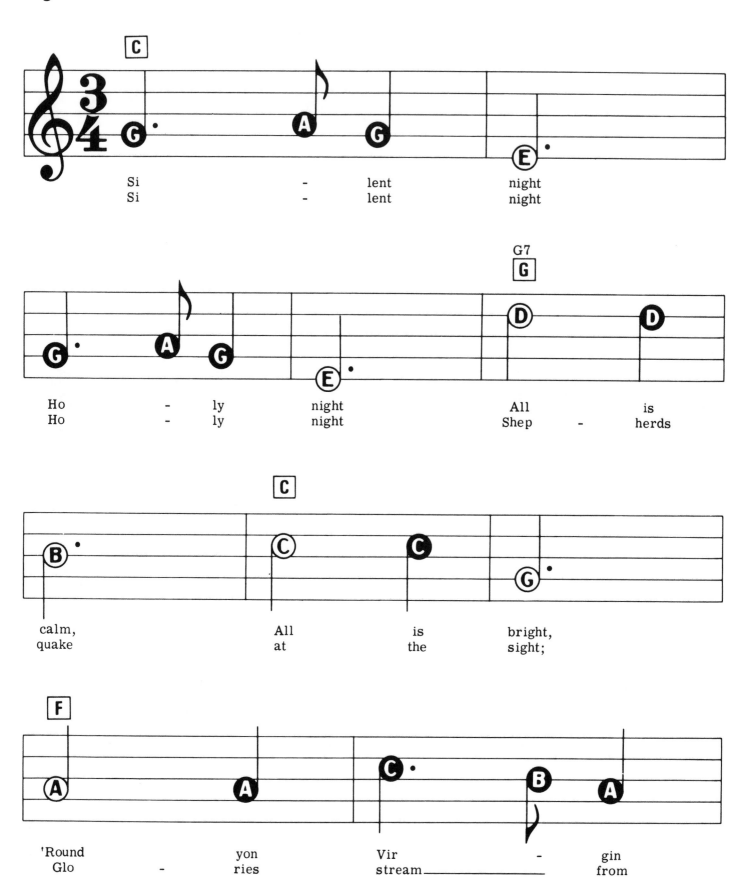

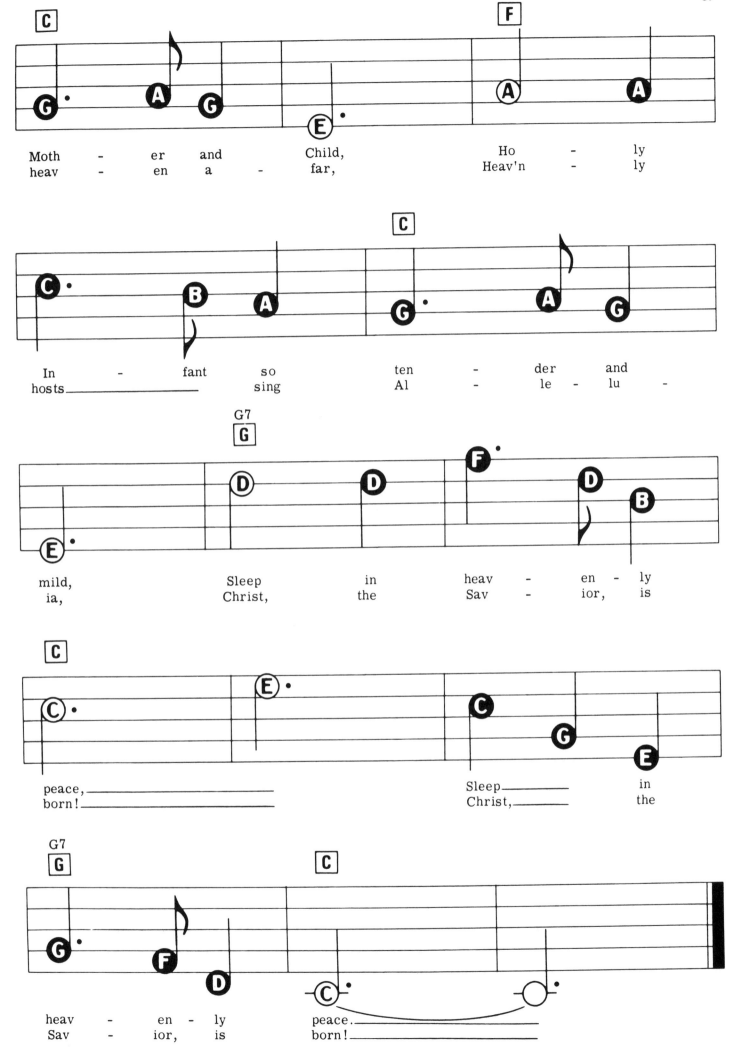

Still, Still, Still

Registration 5

Sing We Now Of Christmas

Registration 2
Rhythm: Ballad or Fox Trot

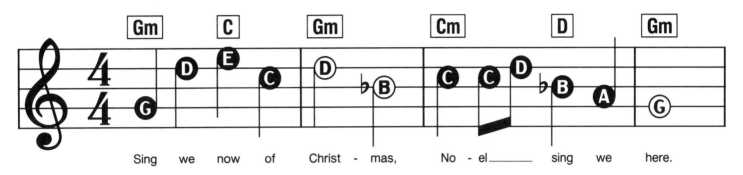

Sing we now of Christ - mas, No - el___ sing we here.

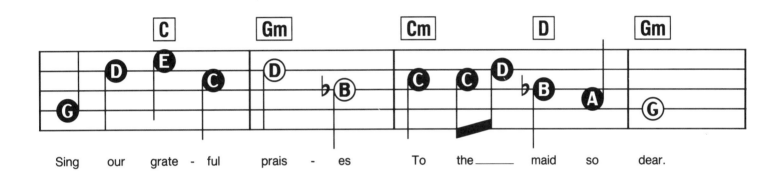

Sing our grate - ful prais - es To the___ maid so dear.

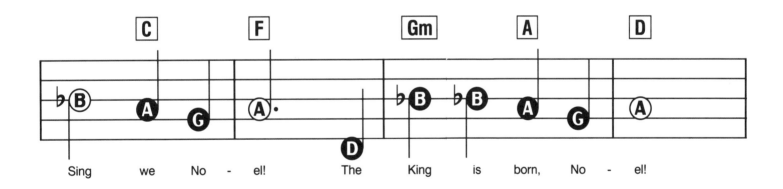

Sing we No - el! The King is born, No - el!

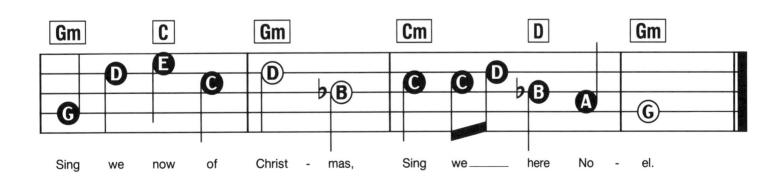

Sing we now of Christ - mas, Sing we___ here No - el.

Up On The Housetop

Registration 5
Rhythm: Fox Trot or Ballad

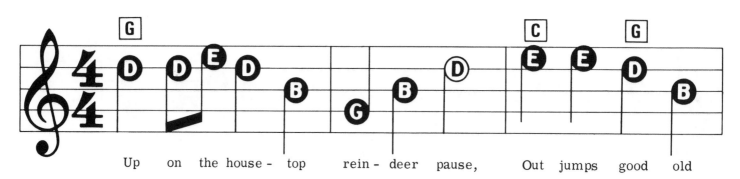

Up on the house - top rein - deer pause, Out jumps good old

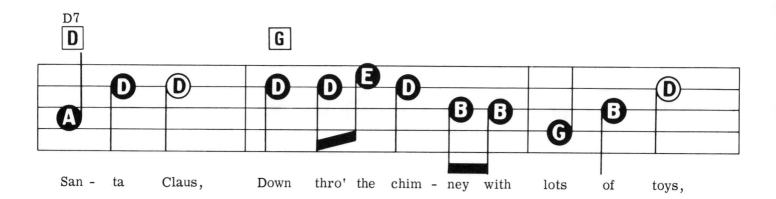

San - ta Claus, Down thro' the chim - ney with lots of toys,

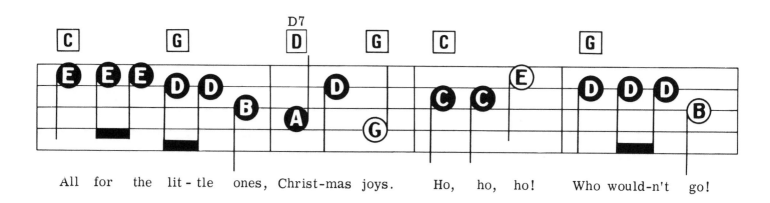

All for the lit - tle ones, Christ-mas joys. Ho, ho, ho! Who would-n't go!

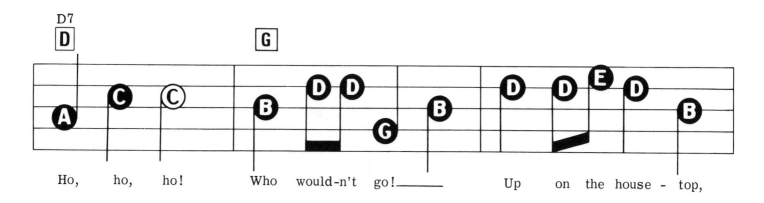

Ho, ho, ho! Who would-n't go!_____ Up on the house - top,

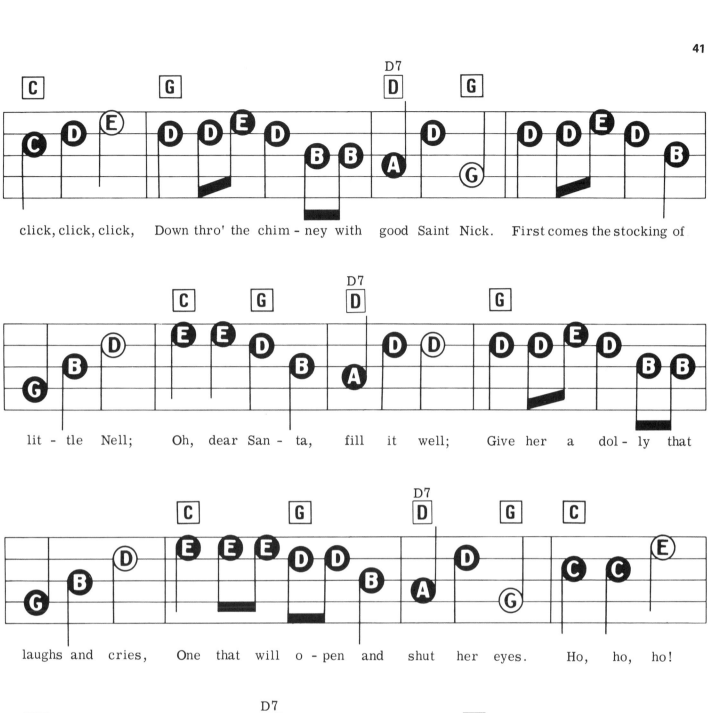

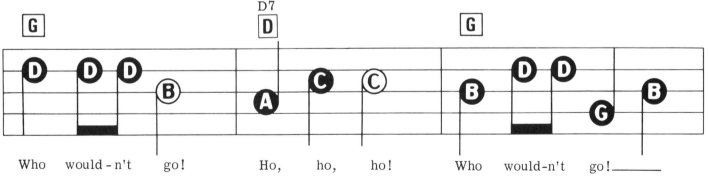

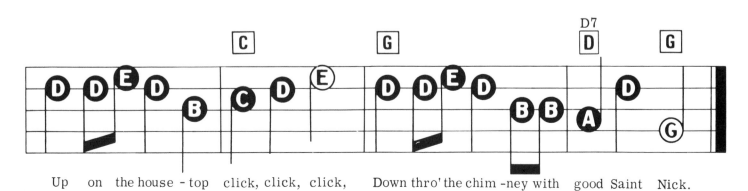

We Three Kings

Registration 9

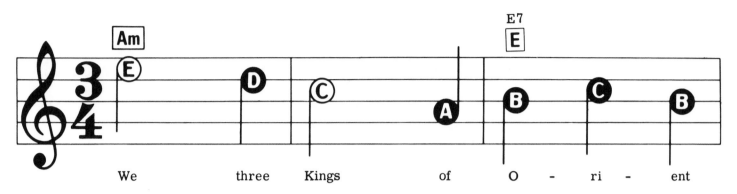

We three Kings of O - ri - ent

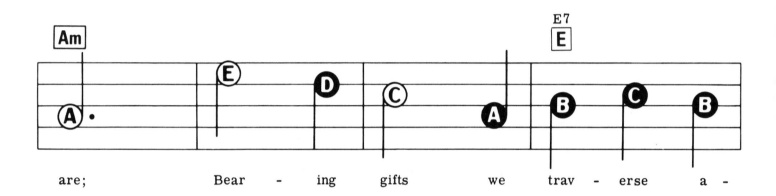

are; Bear - ing gifts we trav - erse a -

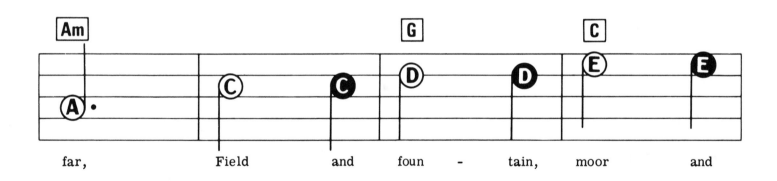

far, Field and foun - tain, moor and

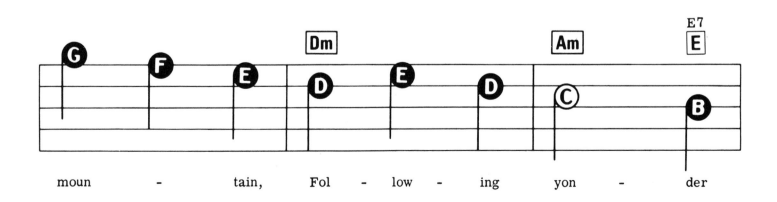

moun - tain, Fol - low - ing yon - der

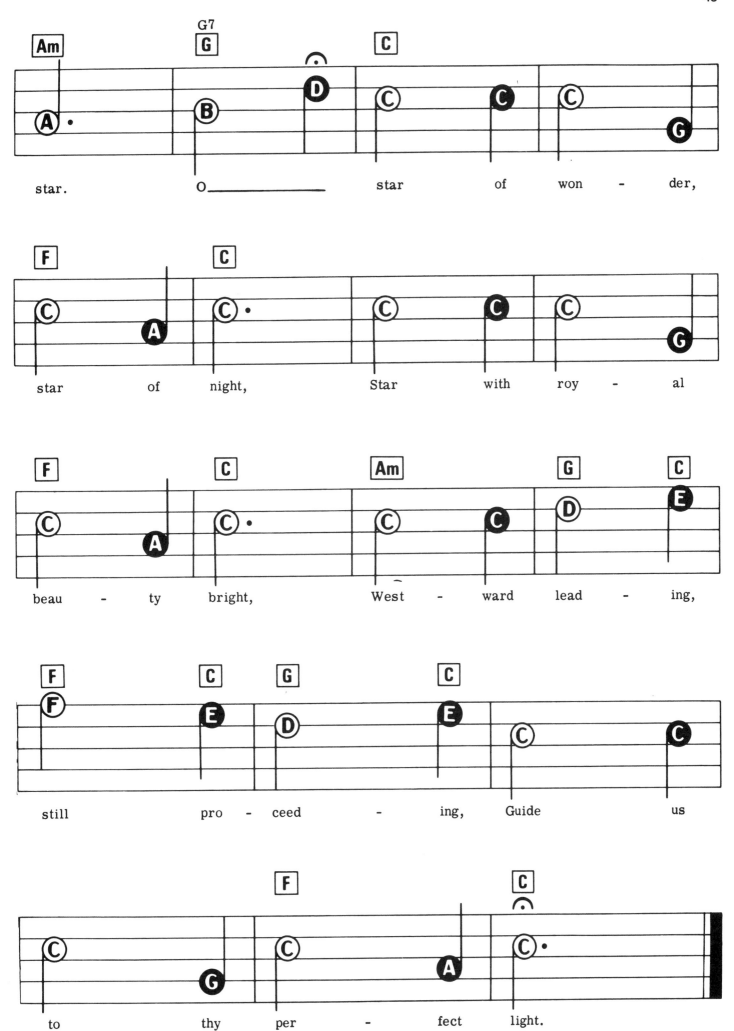

What Child Is This?

Registration 10

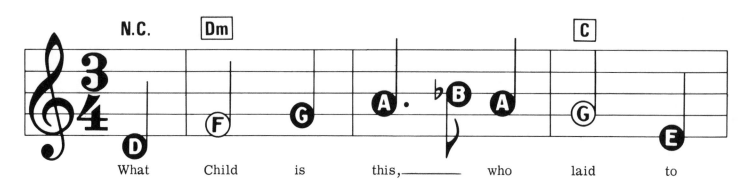

What Child is this,———— who laid to

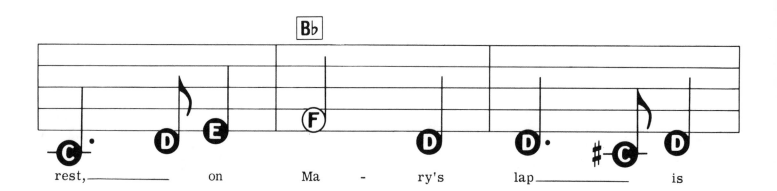

rest,———————— on Ma - ry's lap———————— is

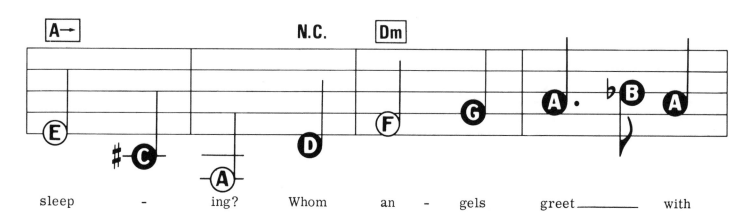

sleep - ing? Whom an - gels greet———— with

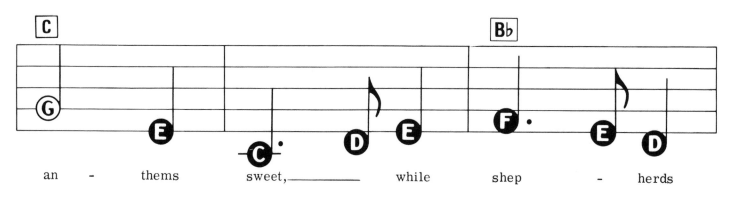

an - thems sweet,———————— while shep - herds

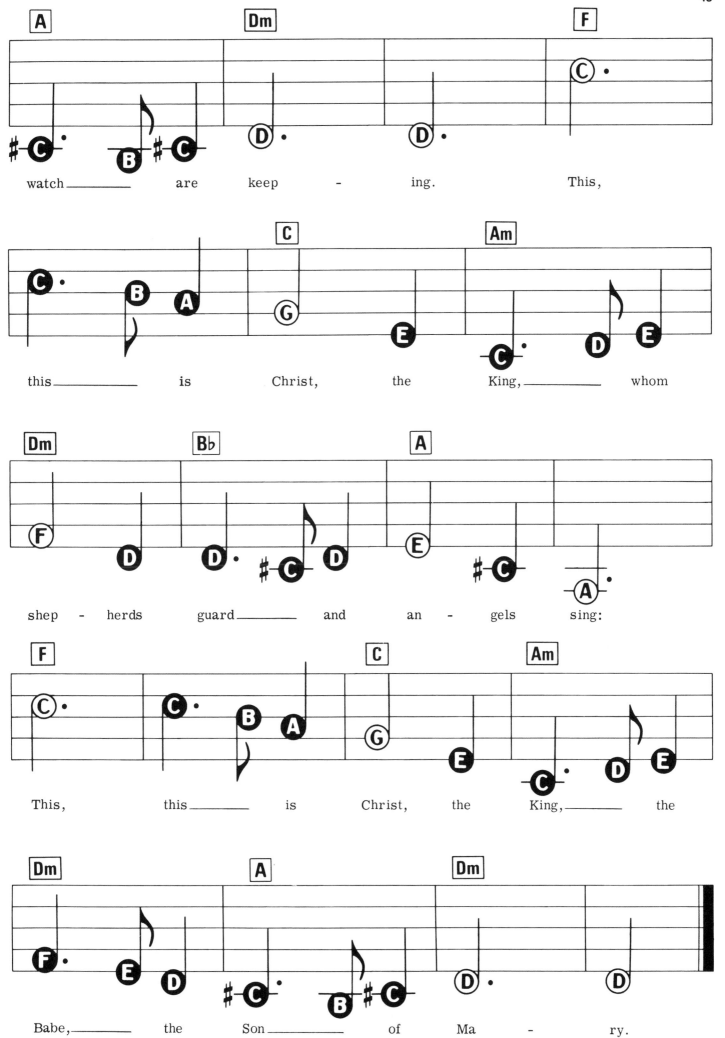

While Shepherds Watched Their Flocks

Registration 1

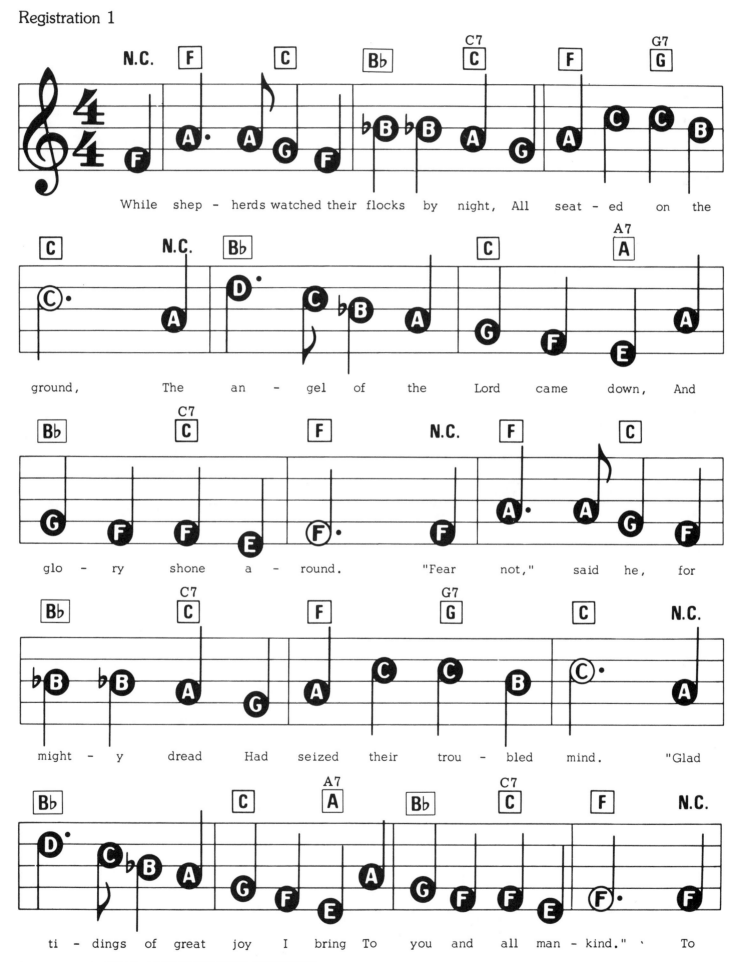

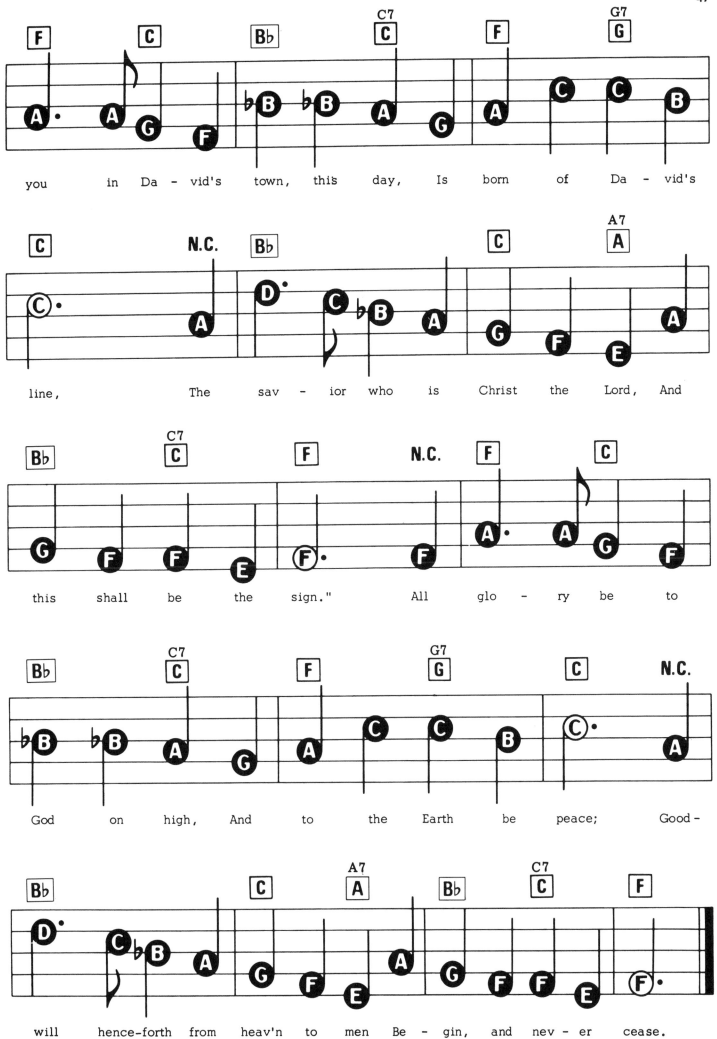

E-Z Play® TODAY Registration Guide
For All Organs

On the following chart are 10 numbered registrations for both tonebar (TB) and electronic tab organs. The numbers correspond to the registration numbers on the E-Z Play TODAY songs. Set up as many voices and controls listed for each specific number as you have available on your instrument. For more detailed registrations, ask your dealer for the E-Z Play TODAY Registration Guide for your particular organ model.

REG. NO.		UPPER (SOLO)	LOWER (ACCOMPANIMENT)	PEDAL	GENERALS
1	Tab	Flute 16', 2'	Diapason 8' Flute 4'	Flute 16', 8'	Tremolo/Leslie – Fast
1	TB	80 0808 000	(00) 7600 000	46, Sustain	Tremolo/Leslie – Fast (Upper/Lower)
2	Tab	Flute 16', 8', 4', 2', 1'	Diapason 8' Flute 8', 4'	Flute 16' String 8'	Tremolo/Leslie – Fast
2	TB	80 7806 004	(00) 7503 000	46, Sustain	Tremolo/Leslie – Fast (Upper/Lower)
3	Tab	Flute 8', 4', 2⅔', 2' String 8', 4'	Diapason 8' Flute 4' String 8'	Flute 16', 8'	Tremolo/Leslie – Fast
3	TB	40 4555 554	(00) 7503 333	46, Sustain	Tremolo/Leslie – Fast (Upper/Lower)
4	Tab	Flute 16', 8', 4' Reed 16', 8'	Flute 8', (4) Reed 8'	Flute 8' String 8'	Tremolo/Leslie – Fast
4	TB	80 7766 008	(00) 7540 000	54, Sustain	Tremolo/Leslie – Fast (Upper/Lower)
5	Tab	Flute 16', 4', 2' Reed 16', 8' String 8', 4'	Diapason 8' Reed 8' String 4'	Flute 16', 8' String 8'	Tremolo/Leslie
5	TB	40 4555 554 Add all 4', 2' voices	(00) 7503 333	57, Sustain	
6	Tab	Flute 16', 8', 4' Diapason 8' String 8'	Diapason 8' Flute 8' String 4'	Diapason 8' Flute 8'	Tremolo/Leslie – Slow (Chorale)
6	TB	45 6777 643	(00) 6604 020	64, Sustain	Tremolo/Leslie – Slow (Chorale)
7	Tab	Flute 16', 8', 5⅓', 2⅔', 1'	Flute 8', 4' Reed 8'	Flute 8' String 8'	Chorus (optional) Perc Attack
7	TB	88 0088 000	(00) 4333 000	45, Sustain	Tremolo/Leslie – Slow (Chorale)
8	Tab	Piano Preset or Flute 8' or Diapason 8'	Diapason 8'	Flute 8'	
8	TB	00 8421 000	(00) 4302 010	43, Sustain	Perc Piano
9	Tab	Clarinet Preset or Flute 8' Reed 16', 8'	Flute 8' Reed 8'	Flute 16', 8'	Vibrato
9	TB	00 8080 840	(00) 5442 000	43, Sustain	Vibrato
10	Tab	String (Violin) Preset or Flute 16' String 8', 4'	Flute 8' Reed 8'	Flute 16', 8'	Vibrato or Delayed Vibrato
10	TB	00 7888 888	(00) 7765 443	57, Sustain	Vibrato or Delayed Vibrato

NOTE: TIBIAS may be used in place of FLUTES. VIBRATO may be used in place of LESLIE.